Christ in the Commandments

A Family Study of the Ten Commandments

By Luke Gilkerson

Christ in the Commandments

By: Luke Gilkerson
Cover Design: Sarah Thomas

Intoxicated on Life • Copyright 2014 Luke Gilkerson

TABLE OF CONTENTS

INTRODUCTION

As parents, there are different ways we can help our children understand the Word of God. The first, and probably most common way, is by giving them a broad understanding of Scripture. By reading through major Bible stories and events, year after year, we give them "the big picture" of the Bible from beginning to end. This is vital for them to develop a Biblical worldview.

Second, we can spend time drilling deep to specific books or passages. We teach our children the value of contemplating a single word or phrase, showing them just how rich the Bible can be. This models for our children the art of studying the Bible in all its fullness and teaches them to pause and reflect all the words God has inspired.

This family devotional is an example of the second way. It will help your children grasp the rich truths contained in Exodus 20:1-21.

HOW TO USE THIS STUDY

There are at least a couple ways you could use this family devotional.

You could spend 30 days in a row, working through one lesson each day. This will immerse your children in the passage.

You could spend 30 weeks doing one lesson each week. You might choose to do this over the duration of one school year.

I would suggest using not one, but both of these approaches, particularly if you will be memorizing this passage of Scripture. Spend 30 days going through this study to acquaint your family with the text prior to memorizing the text. This will help them understand why you are memorizing it. Then, use the Bible study weekly throughout the year to study this Scripture at a slower pace and reinforce the lessons that were already covered once. Repetition is the mother of learning.

Make it a Goal to Memorize

Over the next several months or throughout an entire school year, make a commitment to memorize all of Exodus 20:1-21 as a family.

There is great benefit to memorizing Scripture, and an added benefit to memorizing a lengthier text like this. Memorizing a whole chapter or longer passage gives our children a sense of context. They can begin seeing how to interpret the Bible, seeing how to read a whole section of Scripture in context.

Memory Method: Using Scripture Memory Cards

One of the best ways to move Scripture from short-term to long-term memory is to use a Charlotte Mason-style "memory box."

Become a subscriber at http://intoxicatedonlife.com/freebies/ and you'll get access to free printables. There Exodus 20:1-21 is divided into manageable sections (2-3 verses) on individual index cards.

You'll also find free printable tabbed dividers to help organize all your cards. You'll find...
- A tab marked "Daily"
- A tab marked "Odd Days" and another marked "Even Days"
- Weekly tabs (a tab for each day of the week)
- Monthly tabs (tabs numbered 1-30)

Here's how it works:

1. Place all your tabbed dividers into the box in order.
2. Start by placing the first Philippians card behind the "Daily" tab. Review this card with your child daily, having him or her recite it aloud every day.
3. Once your child can quote an entire card from memory with ease, move it back to either the "odd" tab or "even" tab. Then, only review that card on odd or even dates of the month.
4. Once your child continues to quote the card without help for a couple weeks, move it back to one of the weekly tabs.
5. If they can quote the card several weeks in a row without help, then move it back to one of the monthly tabs.
6. As cards move out from behind the daily tab, add new cards to the daily memory time.

Use Handwriting to Teach

In Deuteronomy 17:18-19, the kings of Israel were commanded to write out for themselves a copy of the law of Moses so that they could read it all the days of their lives. God clearly sees value in not only reading the Bible daily, but also in copying the text of the Bible by hand.

A good way to reinforce Scripture memory (and practice handwriting skills) is to copy Bible passages by hand. **As a companion to this Bible study, you can get a copy of our Exodus 20 version** of *Write Through the Bible*, available at http://intoxicatedonlife.com/product-tag/10-commandments/.

These workbooks take 131 days to complete, about one school year, and combine the disciplines of handwriting, dictation, vocabulary, and Bible memory into one daily activity. The *Write Through the Bible* downloadable workbooks are available in both manuscript and cursive and in either KJV or ESV translations.

How This Study Approaches the Ten Commandments

The Ten Commandments have always served as a mirror for God's people to see their own sinfulness. Next to God's perfect, righteous standards, none of us measure up. As we meditate on the Ten Commandments, our consciences awaken to our need for God's grace. This is one of the primary goals of this study: to help your children see their need for the grace of Christ.

But the Ten Commandments are also a window to see Christ. Jesus lived out the commandments perfectly. Jesus embodies the commandments. In this study, as each commandment is discussed, your kids will learn how each commandment points to Christ, the One we are called to emulate and worship.

A Note About Sabbath Controversies

In this book, I deliberately avoid talking about Sabbath practices and teachings that differ from church to church. The chapters about the fourth commandment do not focus on whether we are obligated to celebrate the Sabbath under the New Covenant, whether we are to do it on Saturday or Sunday, whether Sunday should be considered a "Christian Sabbath," whether the Sabbath should start at sundown or midnight, or what practices and activities should be avoided on the Sabbath.

These are all worthy questions Christian families and churches should address, but in this family devotional, the emphasis is on principles laid down in the Sabbath command: the importance of work, rest, worship, and how the Sabbath is a shadow of the ultimate rest Christ will bring to His people. Families can feel free to supplement the lessons about the Sabbath with teachings from their own church traditions.

A Note About Adultery

The seventh commandment about adultery naturally requires some conversation about marriage and intimacy. This study purposely avoids information about sex, giving discretion to parents about how much or little should be said according to the maturity of their children. Parents can feel free to supplement the conversation with more detailed information about sexual intercourse if they feel the timing is right.

Praying Through Psalm 119

Every lesson ends with a prayer based on the Scriptures. As each commandment is studied (lessons 3-24), I suggest reading through a small portion of Psalm 119 as part of your prayer. You'll see a suggested portion to read aloud during each prayer.

Psalm 119, the longest chapter of the Bible, is a celebration of God's law. It is important for our children not to have a negative perception of law. While the Bible speaks negatively of legalism, in both the Old and New Testaments, God is revealed as a law-giver. As Christians, we follow "the law of Christ" (1 Corinthians 9:21; Galatians 6:2). We follow his commands (John 15:14). As your family prays the text of Psalm 119, your children will sense the overwhelming love the psalmist has for God's law.

Ten Reasons Your Kids Should Memorize the Ten Commandments

There are many texts in the Bible worth memorizing. Why is Exodus 20:1-21 such a good passage learn?

1. **God highlighted the importance of the Ten Commandments by how He gave them to His people.** The giving of the Ten Commandments at Mount Sinai is the one time in human history a large group of people undeniably heard the audible voice of God (Exodus 20:1,19; Deuteronomy 5:4-5, 24-26). They are the only part of Scripture that was literally "hand-written" by God Himself on tablets of stone (Exodus 24:12-13; 31:18; Deuteronomy 9:10). Among all of God's words, the Ten Commandments alone were carried in the Ark of the Covenant (Deuteronomy 10:1-2).

2. **God told parents to constantly remind their children about all the amazing things that were said and done at Mount Sinai during the giving of the Ten Commandments.** The events at Mount Sinai were startling. As God's presence descended on the mountain, fire engulfed the top of Mount Sinai, smoke surrounded it, lightning lit up the sky, thunder rumbled, a great horn blast sounded, and God's own voice shouted to the people. God said He did this "so that they may learn to fear Me all the days that they live on the earth, and that they may teach their children so" (Deuteronomy 4:10). Parents are told to make these things known to their children and grandchildren (4:9). This is exactly what faithful parents in Israel did.

3. **The revelation of God at Mount Sinai inspires us to worship.** Moses' final poetic blessing to Israel begins with, "The Lord came from Sinai...with flaming fire at his right hand" (Deuteronomy 33:2). After one of Israel's great victories, Deborah sang about the God of Israel who shakes the mountains like he shook Sinai (Judges 5:5). Mount Sinai was in the back of many psalmists minds as they wrote of God's majesty and power (Psalm 29:3-4, 7-8; 97:2-5; 144:5). The memory of Mount Sinai is meant to inspire our worship.

4. **The book of Proverbs, written as a guide of parental wisdom for children, has many allusions to the Ten Commandments.** The Proverbs of Solomon speak of honoring one's father and mother (1:8; 23:22-25), not killing (1:10; 6:16-17), not committing adultery (2:16-17; 5:8-23; 6:25-29; 7:1-27), not stealing (10:2; 13:11; 16:8), not giving false witness (6:19; 19:9; 21:28), and not coveting (11:6; 21:26). Similarly, the Ten Commandments can become a foundation for guiding our own children in wisdom.

5. **Jesus taught from the Ten Commandments.** Jesus kept all his Father's commandments (John 15:10). He knew the importance the first two commandments, serving and worshipping God alone (Matthew 4:10). Jesus spoke of the third commandment: the evil of blasphemy (15:19-20). Jesus

obeyed the fourth commandment by honoring the Sabbath day (Matthew 12:11-12; Mark 2:27; Luke 13:14-16). He taught his disciples to honor their parents (Matthew 15:4; 19:19), not be filled with murderous anger (5:21-22; 15:19-20; 19:18), or adulterous lust (5:27-28; 15:19-20; 19:18), not to steal (15:19-20; 19:18; 21:13), not to bear false witness (15:19-20; 19:18), nor covet (Mark 7:22-23). For our children to understand the teachings of Christ, they must have a grasp of the commandments.

6. **The Apostle Paul highlighted their importance.** Paul vividly remembered the day "the commandment came" in his life (Romans 7:9), perhaps learning the law as a child, and this convinced him of his sinfulness (7:7-12). Paul said the latter half of the Ten Commandments are the ways in which we can show love to one another (Romans 13:8-10). Paul highlighted the commandment about honoring one's parents and indicated that God's blessing to obedient children is still promised to Christian children today (Ephesians 6:1-3).

7. **Church leaders from every era have highlighted their importance.** Church leaders from Eastern Orthodox, Roman Catholic, and Protestant traditions all speak to the centrality of the Ten Commandments when it comes to understanding God's moral law. Explanations of the Ten Commandments are part of official confessions and catechisms from many church traditions, used by churches to teach and instruct children in the basics of the faith.

8. **American culture and government has historically honored the wisdom of the Ten Commandments.** Above the entrance to the Supreme Court building in Washington D.C., Moses is etched carrying a tablet of the Law among many other famous lawgivers of ancient history. John Quincy Adams, the sixth President of the United States, said, "The law given from Sinai was a civil and municipal as well as a moral and religious code…laws essential to the existence of men in society and most of which have been enacted by every nation which ever professed any code of laws."

9. **The Ten Commandments serve as good place to start with teaching morality to our children.** There are many views about whether the Old Testament laws are applicable to Christians today. Regardless of your stance on this, the moral precepts mentioned in the Ten Commandments are echoed in the law of Christ and serve as a great place to start in talking with your children about obedience to the Lord.

10. **The Ten Commandments are a great picture of the character of God.** The One who commands us to worship Him alone is a God who seeks His own glory and honor above all other gods. The One who commands us not to kill is the creator of all human life. The One who commands us not to commit adultery is the Always-Faithful One. The One who commands us not to covet is the God who has no need of anything. As parents, we should impress this truth on our children: by memorizing the Ten Commandments they are learning about the nature of God Himself.

Opening Thought:

Have you ever seen a really big thunderstorm? (*Have your kids share a time when they've seen a large storm, either in person, on TV, or in a movie. Ask them to describe how bright the lightning was and how loud the thunder was. Have your kids describe the storm in more vivid detail. If they can't remember a storm, describe one you have seen.*)

In the story we're about to read, God is going to create one of the most powerful storms ever. See if you can picture it in your mind as I read.

Scripture Reading: Exodus 19:9-19 and 20:1-2

Explanation: God tells his servant Moses that the people of Israel need to prepare themselves because He is about to visit them in a powerful way.

If you were about to meet a great and powerful king, you would want to wear your best clothes, not just your normal clothes. You would want to show him how much you respected him. That's what God wanted the Israelites to do: wash their clothes and be ready for His arrival.

God tells Moses to put up a boundary line around Mount Sinai. No one is allowed to approach the mountain, not even animals. This isn't going to be just an ordinary mountain anymore. It is about to become God's throne on Earth. No one is allowed to walk casually on the mountain. If anyone tries to cross the boundary line, Moses is instructed to kill the person immediately by shooting an arrow or stone at him.

Three days later, as the sun rises, they hear it: the sound of thunder. Everyone comes out of their tents and start walking toward the mountain. Gathering around the top of the mountain are thick, dark storm clouds. They can see the lightning getting brighter and hear the thunder getting louder. The entire mountain is covered in darkness. Behind the clouds they can see the mountain engulfed in flames. God has come down on the mountain, cloaked in fire, and the smoke from the fire mixes with the clouds. As the people get closer, they can feel the ground shaking violently. They also hear the sound of a loud trumpet blast. Like a king who has trumpeters announce his presence when he walks into a room, God is announcing His arrival.

Imagine the scene: the fire, the smoke, the dark clouds, the lightning, the thunder, the trumpet blast, the shaking ground. The Bible says as the people approach, they also start shaking. Have you ever been so scared that you physically shook? That's how scared they are.

Then they hear it: God's voice begins speaking. This is the only time in the whole Bible where God gathers a large group of people to listen to His voice out loud. Usually He speaks to prophets and they speak to the people for Him. Not this time. This time, God talks to the people Himself.

Questions for Your Kids:

1. How do think you would have felt standing at the foot of the mountain? (*Have your kids describe how they would feel? If they don't know, remind them just how destructive and powerful things like fire and lightning are.*)

2. Why do you think God is showing up in this powerful way? (*Have your kids think about why. Later on we learn it is because God wants them to fear Him and revere Him. He wants them to remember this day forever. God is great and powerful and can judge our sin, so we should treat Him with deep respect.*)

3. Did the people actually get to see God that day? (*No. They only saw the mountain wrapped in smoke and clouds. They only heard His voice.*)

4. If this is the only time in the Bible that God speaks out loud to a big group of people, do you think He's about to say something really important? (*Yes. Whatever God is about to say should really catch our attention.*)

Prayer: Your Word says that clouds and thick darkness are all around You. Righteousness and justice are the foundation of Your throne. Fire goes before You and burns up Your enemies on every side. Your lightning lights up the world; the earth sees and trembles. The mountains melt like wax before You. You are the Lord of all the earth (Psalm 97:1-5). You spoke from the midst of the fire on Mount Sinai. People heard it and lived to tell about it (Deuteronomy 4:32-33). We want to learn what You said. Help us to learn to fear You and respect You as they did. Amen.

Opening Thoughts:

Do you know what slavery is? (*Slavery is when someone owns another person and forces them to work.*)

Do you think being a slave would be hard? What do you think the worst part would be? (*Have your kids think about what worst parts of being a slave could be. Would it be the bad food? Being treated like property? No freedom? Working long hours?*)

Do you know that before the people of Israel got to Mount Sinai, they used to be slaves? (*If your kids can recall anything about that story, have them do it. Israel had been in slavery in Egypt for about 400 years. They made bricks in the hot sun for the Pharaohs. They were beaten with rods and whips. On one occasion, all their babies were drowned in the Nile River.*)

Remember that story as we read these couple verses.

Scripture Reading: Exodus 19:16-19 and 20:1-3

Explanation: Why would God introduce Himself, saying, "I am God"? With all the smoke, fire, lightning, thunder, and loud trumpet blast, isn't it obvious to them that He must be God? But God isn't just saying that He is God. He is reminding them what kind of God He is and what He has done for them.

God tells them His name: the Lord. Actually, that's just a translation. In the original language, His name is Yahweh. It is the name God gave Himself. The name means, "I am who I am," or it also means, "I will be who I will be." God named Himself Yahweh because He has always existed, He will always exist, He is Lord over everything, and He doesn't need anything from anyone. That is the kind of God He is.

He is also the God who brought them up out of the land of Egypt. When they were enslaved by the Egyptians, He heard their prayers and came to rescue them. He sent Moses to them and performed great wonders and miracles in Egypt. Little by little, He destroyed Egypt until Pharaoh let Israel go. God rescued them from slavery in a powerful way.

This is important to know. God doesn't start by giving them a bunch of rules to follow. He starts by reminding them **who He is** and **who they are**. Who is He? The all-powerful Creator who rescued them. Who are they? They once were slaves, but now they are God's own special people. He's not saying, "Here are my laws. If you obey them, then I'll love you." No. He's saying, "I have shown my love to you. I have saved you. You are already my people. Now here's how I want my people to live."

Questions for Your Kids:

1. Do you know that all people on earth are slaves of something? Can you guess what it is? (*We are all slaves of sin. That means we all sin, we all want to sin, and we all can't stop sinning without God's help. Sin is like a cruel slave master. He tells us what to do, and we obey him.*)

2. Who do you think came to rescue us from our slavery to sin? (*Jesus Christ. When we become Christians, the Spirit of Christ comes to live inside us and He frees us from sin. This doesn't mean we become perfect, but it does mean we no longer have to obey our old master Sin anymore. We are free to live differently than we did before.*)

3. Who is our new Master? (*God is our new Lord. We are called to obey Him now.*)

4. Would it be possible for us to obey God's laws if we were still slaves to Sin? (*No. Slaves have to obey their master, and if we are slaves to Sin, we could not obey God.*)

5. Can a Christian obey God's laws? (*Yes. We cannot always obey them perfectly, but we can now learn to obey God because we don't have to do what Sin tells us anymore.*)

6. What if we screw up and don't obey God? Does that mean God doesn't love us anymore? (*No. If we don't obey God, we can ask for His forgiveness and He will forgive us. If He loved us when we were slaves of Sin, when we didn't even want God, then He will surely love us when He has rescued us from Sin.*)

Prayer: Thank you for giving us your love and favor before You give us your law. Thank you for loving us and saving us from sin so that we can be free to follow You. We want to obey You, not as slaves, but as your beloved children (Romans 8:14-15). Thank you for saving us by your grace, not because of anything we've done, but because of what You've done for us. Thank you for making us new creations, meant to do works and follow your law (Ephesians 2:8-10). Amen.

Opening Thought:

What are some of the things you really enjoy? What are some of your favorite things? (*Have your kids list some of their favorite games, activities, experiences, toys, books, TV shows, or anything that is a favorite of theirs.*)

I also have things that are my favorites. (*List three or four things that are your favorites.*)

Keep those things in mind as we read God's first commandment.

Scripture Reading: Exodus 20:1-3

Explanation: Back in Moses' day, people all around the world worshipped different gods. People believed in all kinds of gods that controlled different things. People believed there were gods who controlled the rain, the sunshine, and the stars. They believed there were gods who could help the crops to grow, give women babies, help win battles in war, and the list goes on and on. Of course, none of these gods are real, and if any of them are real, they are not gods at all, but evil spirits trying to steal worship away from the only true God.

The reason why people worshipped these other gods is because of what these gods promise to give them. If you really wanted to have children, you would be tempted to find a god that promised more children. If you really wanted to win a war, you would be tempted to worship a god who promised victory in war.

What they were *really* worshipping were not just these gods, but what the gods promised to give them. That's what they *really* wanted. They wanted what the gods promised so much they were willing to worship these other gods to get them.

Here's another way to think about the idea of "worship." To worship something means we desire it more than anything else in the world. It means we make lots of sacrifices for it: we're willing to spend lots of time and money and energy to get it. We worship something when it is the first thing on our mind, our greatest love, our greatest desire.

In the first commandment, God says, "You shall have no other gods before me." This means God should be our first love, the thing we desire more than anything else. This means we shouldn't desire something more than God. We shouldn't worship God *plus* other things. We must remember, God sees everything, even the desires of our hearts. He knows if we desire something more than Him.

Questions for Your Kids:

1. Think of some of those favorite things I mentioned. If I had to think of anything that I'm most tempted to worship it would be... (*Name one or two things that, if you were really honest, you are most tempted to worship.*)

2. What do you think you are most tempted to worship? (*Help your kids with this if it seems difficult for them to answer. Ask them other probing questions: What are you most afraid of losing? What do you find yourself daydreaming about? What makes you really upset when you don't get your way? What do you pray for most? What makes you happiest? What do I want to have more than anything else? These questions might help your kids think about their greatest desires.*)

3. Why do you think God made this commandment the *first* one? (*God put this commandment first because it's about putting Him first, before anything else: before friends, family, toys, games...anything.*)

Prayer: (Start your prayer by reading Psalm 119:1-8.)
We want to praise You with an upright heart. Thank You for the first commandment that reminds us to put You first. Help us to know the difference between *liking* something and *worshipping* it. Search us, God, and know our thoughts. Know our hearts. Tell us if we worship anything in our hearts (Psalm 139:23-24; Ezekiel 14:4). We want to make You our greatest love. Amen.

LESSON 4:
The First Commandment (Part 2)

Opening Thought:

Remember what we said before about worship. Worshipping something means we desire it more than anything else in the world. We worship something when it is the first thing on our mind, our greatest love, our greatest treasure. People worship false gods because these gods make promises, and people want what they promise more than anything else.

Keep that in mind as we read the first commandment and a couple other passages of Scripture.

Scripture Reading: Exodus 20:1-3, Matthew 4:8-11, and Hebrews 5:7

Explanation: The devil made Jesus a big promise. He would give Jesus all the nations of the world. All Jesus had to do was bow down and worship Satan just one time. But Jesus didn't do it. Jesus quoted part of the Bible that he had memorized about how God is the only One we should worship and serve. Yes, Satan made Jesus a big promise, but Jesus knew His Father was better than that promise.

Jesus knew He was the Messiah, the Son of God, and that His Father was going to give Him the kingdoms of the world some day. One day, Jesus would be made King over the whole world. Satan was offering Jesus a shortcut, a way to become the King early. But Jesus knew better. He trusted that His Father's way was the best way. Although Jesus was tempted by the devil, He chose to put His Father first.

The Bible says that when Jesus was on Earth, He revered and worshipped His Father. He trusted His Father with everything. He loved praying to His Father. He loved His Father more than anything in the world. Jesus obeyed the first commandment perfectly.

But we don't obey the first commandment like Jesus did. We are all tempted to make other people or things more important than God. There are days when God is not on our mind at all. But Jesus was perfect, and when He died for our sins on the cross, He was the *perfect* sacrifice. This is why we are forgiven for every time we sin against God and don't put Him first.

Questions for Your Kids:

1. Is there anything that should be more enjoyable to us than God? (*No. God should be our first love.*)

2. Did Jesus ever break the first commandment? (*No. Christ was perfect. He loved His Father more than anything.*)

3. What can we do to remember to worship God throughout the day? (*We can strive to be more like Christ. We can read about Christ and be inspired by how much He loved God. We can memorize Scripture like Jesus did and recite it when we are tempted to put something else before God.*)

Prayer: (Start your prayer by reading Psalm 119:9-16.)
Thank You, Christ, for always putting Your Father first. Thank You for being the perfect sacrifice for our sins so we can be forgiven every time we fail to put God first. Your obedience to God inspires us to love God. Help us to hide Your Word in our hearts so we do not sin against You. Amen.

Opening Thought:

Do you remember what the Israelites saw and heard when they were standing at the foot of Mount Sinai when God came down to meet them? (*Have your kids describe what they remember about the thunder, lightning, fire, smoke, trumpet blast, and God's voice.*)

Were they actually able to **see** God? (*No. God did not visibly show Himself. They saw no form of God that day; they only heard His voice.*)

If someone wanted to make a statue of God based on what they saw that day on Mount Sinai, they couldn't do it because God never showed them what He looks like. Keep that in mind as we read God's second commandment.

Scripture Reading: Exodus 20:4-6

Explanation: When the other nations around Israel wanted to worship their false gods, they would often carve images of those gods out of stone or wood. These were called idols. But God tells Israel, "When you worship Me, don't worship **Me** that way. Don't make an idol that is supposed to represent Me or any other god."

The first commandment is about **who** we should worship. The second commandment is about **how** we should worship. The first commandment tells us to worship and love God above everything else. The second commandment tells us the **way** God wants to be worshipped. We may worship the correct God, but we need to worship Him the correct way.

The reason people make idols is because they want to make the gods they worship into what **they** want. They want to make a god that they prefer. They want to make a god that looks the way they want it to look. They want a god they can control.

You've probably never tried to carve a statue of God out of stone or wood, but we can all make idols of God **in our minds**. This when we think about God the wrong way. This is when we make worshipping God all about **us** and what **we** want.

Think about it: When you go to church to worship God, do you ever say to yourself, "I really don't like singing that music"? Or do you say, "I wish this sermon would be over so I can do something fun"? Or do you think, "I wish they would say something interesting"? There's nothing wrong with liking good music or good speaking, but when we think worshipping God should be about what *we* want or what *we* like, we are forgetting that worship is all about *God*. We are forgetting how big and amazing God really is.

Or think about this: When we worry about something over and over, we are really saying in our mind, "I don't think God can take care of this problem I'm having." When we do this we have an image of God in our mind that is wrong: we believe God isn't big enough or strong enough or loving enough to help us. The god we are imagining in our mind is too small or too far away to do anything about our problem. This is an idol in our minds. But the real God is big enough and close enough to handle anything. He is always in control.

Questions for Your Kids:

1. What is an idol? (*An idol is a picture or carved image that is supposed to represent a god.*)

2. How do we make idols in our minds? (*We make idols in our minds when we think things about God that aren't true or we worship God in a selfish way.*)

3. When we are at church worshipping God, instead of asking, "Did I like the stuff that happened at church today?" what should we be thinking? (*We should be thinking about whether God was pleased with our worship.*)

Prayer: (Start your prayer by reading Psalm 119:17-24.)

You have opened our eyes so that we can see wondrous things in Your law. Forgive us when we make idols in our minds. We have been guilty of thinking You are smaller than You really are. But really, Your greatness and wisdom are unsearchable (Psalm 145:3; Romans 11:33). Your love surpasses anything we can know (Ephesians 3:18-19). No one can grasp how powerful you are (Job 26:14). Your mercies never come to an end (Lamentations 3:22-23). You can do far more than all we can ever ask or imagine (Ephesians 3:20). Amen.

Opening Thought:

If a man and a woman are married but then another man comes along who wants to get married to that same woman, does the first man, her husband, feel jealous? (*Yes. Have your kids describe what jealousy feels like. Jealousy is when we don't want anything to come between us and the one we love.*)

If there is only one child in a family and then a new baby brother or sister comes along, can the first kid sometimes get jealous of all the attention the new baby gets? (*Yes. Sometimes kids can be jealous for a parent's attention.*)

As we read the second commandment again, be listening for the word "jealous." We'll also read a passage about Jesus.

Scripture Reading: Exodus 20:4-6 and Colossians 1:15-17

Explanation: Remember what an idol is. An idol is an image we make of a god. It can be an image we make of a false god, or an image we try to make of the real God. This can be something we make out of wood or stone, but it could also be a wrong idea about God in our mind. God never wanted Israel to make idols with their hands or in their minds.

God says He is a jealous God. As Christians, we belong to God. He doesn't want us to have a wrong idea about who He is. He is jealous for His own glory. He wants His people to know who He *really* is. When we have a wrong idea about God in our mind, it is getting in the way of us worshipping the real God.

Many hundreds of years after Moses gave the Ten Commandments, God did something amazing to show us who He *really* is. God's Son, Jesus Christ, came to earth as a man. He was perfect in every way. He taught people the truth, He healed their diseases, He fed them, He had compassion on them, and He did many miracles that showed how big God is. He even conquered death by rising from the dead after He was crucified.

The Bible says Jesus is the *image* of the invisible God. We aren't allowed to make images of God, but God has already given us an image of what He is like. He sent Jesus to us. Before Jesus, God had spoken through many, many prophets about who He is. He had done many miracles and wonders to show us who He is. But if we want the clearest picture of who God is, we can look at the person of Jesus. God is invisible, but Jesus shows us what the invisible God is like.

Questions for Your Kids:

1. If someone were to ask you what the second commandment was, what would you say? (*See how much of the text of Exodus 20:4-6 they can remember or if they can paraphrase what it says.*)

2. Is God visible or invisible? (*Invisible. We cannot see Him.*)

3. Who was the image of the invisible God? (*Jesus, God's Son*)

4. What does it mean that Jesus was the image of the invisible God? (*Jesus show us what God is like.*)

5. Knowing that Jesus is the image of God, the next time we are with God's people worshipping God, what is something we can be thinking about that will help us to be excited about God? (*We can think about what we know about Jesus. We can think about the stories from Jesus' life. We can think about the way He showed His love, power, compassion, and joy to others. We can think about His death on the cross for our sins. We can think about His resurrection. We can think about how He's going to come again to earth.*)

6. Worship isn't something we just do when we gather as the church. Worship is something we do in our hearts all week long. Can thinking about Christ throughout the week help us to worship God more? (*Yes. We can think about and remember Christ all week long.*)

Prayer: (Start your prayer by reading Psalm 119:25-32.)
Thank you for sending us Jesus. He is the one who shines and reflects Your glory. He shows us exactly what You are like (Hebrews 1:3). He is Your Word made flesh (John 1:14). Help us to obey Your second commandment. Get rid of all wrong images of who You are from our minds. Help us to think more about Jesus Christ. As we think about Jesus, enlarge our hearts so we can worship You more. Amen.

Opening Thought:

Have you ever been to a funeral? (*Have your kids tell you if they have ever been to one. If they haven't, talk about one you have been to.*)

A funeral can be very sad. Sometimes people cry because they miss the person who died. Think about how sad you would be if someone you loved died.

But what would happen if you came to a funeral and instead of being quiet and respectful, you were running around, yelling, and playing? What if you were talking to the crying people, telling them they were being silly for crying so hard? (*That would be very disrespectful to the family of the person who died. There are times when it is very important to be serious, not silly.*)

Think about that as we read God's third commandment.

Scripture Reading: **Exodus 20:7**

Explanation: God says we should not misuse His name or take His name in vain. This means we shouldn't treat God's name lightly. It's like the story about being silly at the funeral: we would be treating the funeral lightly, as if it isn't important or as if it isn't serious. That's what it means to take God's name in vain: it's when we talk about God or use His name in a way that makes it sound like He's not important.

God is important. Think about how big and powerful and holy God is. He has always existed. No one created Him; He is the creator of everything. He is so powerful, He could destroy the entire universe with a single word. God is everywhere. We can never get away from Him. We can never hide from Him. God knows everything. He knows everything that has ever happened and will happen. He is also holy, which means He is set apart and different than anything we know. Nothing and no one is like God. God is so amazing, we can never imagine how great He is.

This is why whenever we say God's name or talk about God, we need to remember who we are talking about. Don't just say the name "God" or "Lord" or "Jesus" like you say any other name. Don't treat His name like a common thing. When we talk to God or we sing songs to God, we shouldn't be thinking about something else or letting our mind wander. Whenever His name is on our lips, we should be thinking about how amazing He is.

We also need to remember that we are named after Christ. We call ourselves "Christians," which means "follower of Christ." If we act in a way that is rude or mean or disrespectful or offensive, others might start to think, "Those Christians aren't very kind. Why would I want to follow Christ?" We never want to give God a bad name.

Questions for Your Kids:

1. When you hear someone say the name of your best friend, what do you think about? (*Have your kids think of who their best friend is and what comes into their mind when they hear that name. Do they think about what the person looks like? What they like to do for fun? What does their voice sound like? The point is this: When we say someone's name we think about that person and what his or she is like.*)

2. So when we think about God's name, what should come into our minds? (*We should think about the amazing things God has said and done. We should think about the kind of God He is.*)

3. Have you ever said God's name, either when you were talking or praying or singing, but you were thinking about something else? (*It's normal for our minds to be thinking about something when we are talking about something else. But when we are talking to or about God, our minds need to concentrate on Him.*)

Prayer: (Start your prayer by reading Psalm 119:33-40.)

How majestic is Your name in all the earth (Psalm 8:1). We want your name to be famous throughout the world (Isaiah 26:8). Everywhere the sun shines, Your name should be praised (Psalm 113:3). You are a God merciful and gracious, slow to anger, and abounding in steadfast love and faithfulness (Exodus 24:6). We want to observe Your law with our whole heart, so help us to honor Your name. Amen.

Opening Thought:

Do you remember what we said about the third commandment? It had something to do with God's name. Can you remember? (*See how much your children can remember from the last lesson.*)

When we are talking to God or about God, we need to remember exactly who we are talking about. We ought to speak God's name with honor because God's greatness cannot be measured. He is amazing.

When Jesus was on earth, He taught us about how we should think about God's name when we pray. Listen as we read the third commandment and as we read the words of Jesus.

Scripture Reading: Exodus 20:7 and Luke 11:1-4

Explanation: Jesus loved to pray. He loved to talk to His Father in heaven. Jesus would often rise up early in the morning just to pray. Sometimes He would pray late at night or stay up all night praying. That's how much He loved His Father.

One day His disciples saw Him praying, and they wanted to learn how to talk to God, too. So Jesus gave them an example prayer. He said when we talk to God, these are the things we should be thinking about. And do you know what the very first thing He had them pray about was? God's name: just like in the third commandment.

Jesus told them to pray, "Hallowed be Your name." This is asking God to make His name holy throughout all the earth. God is already holy. He is the creator of all things. He is perfect in every way. He is bigger, greater, and wiser than anyone else. But not everyone *knows* or *believes* how great God is. There are many people throughout the world who have never even heard about the true God.

That's what Jesus wants us to pray for: that everyone will know the name of God, that everyone will know and love God. But before the whole world believes how amazing God is, first *we* have to believe it. *We* need to obey the third commandment. We need to treat God as holy and wonderful. We need to speak about how wonderful God is. Then we can tell others about Him.

Questions for Your Kids:

1. What is the first thing Jesus wanted His disciples to pray about? (*"Hallowed be Your name"* is the first petition of the Lord's Prayer.)

2. What does "Hallowed be Your name" mean? (*It means, "May Your name be regarded as holy." It means we want to see the rest of the world believe how amazing God is.*)

3. Do you think this is what Jesus prayed for when He prayed? (*Yes. He wanted to see the whole world worshipping His Father in heaven.*)

4. How does this prayer relate to the third commandment? (*The third commandment says we shouldn't take God's name lightly. This prayer says we want God's name to be regarded as holy in all the earth. The third commandment is all about how we shouldn't treat God's name. But the Lord's Prayer tells us how we should treat God's name.*)

Prayer: (Start your prayer by reading Psalm 119:41-48.)

We want all kings and all nations to hear about Your testimonies. Hallowed be Your name. Make Your name holy in the whole earth. We want You to reign over the whole world (Luke 11:2). Help us to treat your name as holy when we speak to You or about You. Amen.

Opening Thought:

How many days are in a week? (*Seven*)

Why do we have seven days in a week? Why not 5 or 10 or any other number? (*See if your children can guess any reason why we would have seven days.*)

The reason why we have seven days in a week goes all the way back to when the world was created by God. I'm going to read two passages. The first is about when God created the world, and the next is the fourth commandment.

Scripture Reading: Genesis 2:1-8, 15 and Exodus 20:8-11

Explanation: According to the first book of the Bible, God created the whole world in six days. He created light, the land, the sea, the sun, the moon, the animals on the land and the sky and the sea, and finally human beings. Then on the seventh day He rested. Then, He set apart the seventh day: He made it holy. He marked the seventh day as special.

When God made human beings, He made us to mimic Him. Just like God, we are supposed to work. God put the first man in the Garden of Eden to work the ground, to help the land grow food. We are meant to do something useful with our time and our energy. We have the power to be creative, just like God. We are all called to work, not be lazy. We all have a calling in life, making this world a beautiful place. We all have work we are meant to do that will bless the world.

But just like God, we are also supposed to rest. God made the seventh day the Sabbath. The word "sabbath" means "intermission" or "making rest." God wants us to stop, rest, and enjoy what we've made. This rest isn't just about taking a day off, but taking time to praise God. It is a Sabbath "to the Lord."

The fourth commandment told the people of Israel to work six days and rest one. Work six days, rest one. This was the pattern. Work hard for six days, and then take one day to rest and thank God. The whole household was to rest: moms, dads, kids, servants, guests living in your house, even animals. The Sabbath was God's gift to them: a day of rest, enjoyment, blessing, and worship.

Questions for Your Kids:

1. Is work a good thing or a bad thing? (*A good thing. God made people to work when the world was perfect, even before there was sin in the world. We are made to do useful work.*)

2. Have you ever thought about what kind of work you will be doing when you are an adult? What do you think? (*Have your kids think about the job they would like to do as an adult. Make suggestions based on what their natural strengths are.*)

3. Why is it important to rest from work? (*We should rest so we can both enjoy what we've created and so we can remember God. Work can take our minds off of God, but if we set aside time to rest, we can pause and remember God who made us and worship Him.*)

Prayer: (Start your prayer by reading Psalm 119:49-56.)

It is good to give thanks to You, to sing praises to Your name (Psalm 92:1). You set apart the seventh day as holy. Help us to set aside time every week to remember that You are the Lord who sanctifies us—You are the God who makes us holy (Exodus 31:13). You made the Sabbath for us (Mark 2:27). Help us to delight in it. We take comfort when we remember Your laws. Amen.

LESSON 10:
The Fourth Commandment (Part 2)

Opening Thought:

Do you remember what God's law about the Sabbath is? (*God gave Israel the Sabbath law. One day in every seven days they were to rest from their labor and spend the day enjoying God and the gifts He had given them.*)

How many days did God take to create the world? (*Six days. He rested on the seventh.*)

The Sabbath day was a gift God gave to His people. But the Sabbath points to something even better. Let's read a couple passages from the New Testament about this.

Scripture Reading: Hebrews 4:4, 9-10 and Matthew 11:28-30

Explanation: God created the world in six days. He rested on the seventh. On the eighth day, He didn't start creating all over again. No, God in heaven has been resting from His creating activities for a long time. This is what God's home in heaven is like: it is a place of eternal rest.

When Jesus comes back, it will be like a never-ending Sabbath. There will be no more sin. We will relax and enjoy God forever.

When God gave His people the law about the Sabbath, it was pointing to something much bigger and better than just one day of rest every seven days. Heaven is a place of rest, and He wants to share that rest with us. There is a day when heaven will come to Earth, and we will live in a Sabbath day that will never end.

We will rest from the worries of this life. We will rest from all the pains of this life: no more tears, no more crying. We will rest from the fear of death: there will be no more dying or illness or sickness. We will rest from sin: we won't want to sin anymore, but we will serve God with our whole heart.

Questions for Your Kids:

1. What do you think heaven will be like? (*Have your kids describe what it will be like. Steer their thoughts toward the best part of heaven: being at rest and enjoying God Himself. It will be an eternal Sabbath.*)

2. Jesus promises rest for our souls. When He returns, what kind of rest will He give to us? Will we just nap the whole time? (*No. It isn't that kind of rest. We will rest from sin and all the effects of sin in this life: illness, worry, pain, and death.*)

3. Do you ever wonder if you will go to heaven? (*See if your kids have ever thought about whether they will or will not go to heaven. If they don't know, talk to them about the gift of salvation they can have through Christ.*)

Prayer: (Start your prayer by reading Psalm 119:57-64.)
You have given the Sabbath as a shadow new world to come, a world of rest (Colossians 2:16-17), and we look forward to the day we will enter Your rest forever (Psalm 95:11). Help us to always cling to Your word so we can trust in You all our lives. Amen.

Opening Thought:

How many laws do you think there are in the Bible? (*Have your kids make a guess.*)

When you count up all the things God says to do or not do, there are hundreds of laws. But God helps us by telling us the most important one. Do you know what the greatest commandment is?

Here's what Jesus had to say about that.

Scripture Reading: Mark 12:28-31

Explanation: This scribe wanted to know what the greatest commandment was. Of all the laws in the Old Testament, what was the most important?

To answer His question, Jesus quotes a passage from one of Moses' last sermons. Right after Moses got finished reciting the Ten Commandments and reminding the Israelites about what they saw at Mount Sinai, Moses says these great words, the most important law in the whole Bible: love the Lord your God with all your heart, soul, mind, and might.

Think of the first four of the Ten Commandments we've studied so far. These first four commands all relate to the greatest commandment Jesus talked about.

1. We shouldn't worship anything or anyone other than God. God should be our first love and our greatest treasure.
2. We shouldn't make an idol. God doesn't want us to be worshipped that way. We shouldn't be selfish and try to make God look the way we want Him to look or make Him be what we want Him to be. He is bigger and greater than that.
3. We shouldn't take God's name in vain. God's name should never be treated lightly. God is great and awesome and powerful, and when we talk to Him or about Him, we should remember that.
4. God made the Sabbath day as a special day to rest from work and remember Him and all the good things He's done.

These first four commands all relate to the greatest commandment. If we love God with all our heart and soul and mind and strength, then we will not want to worship anything else. If we love God, we will want to know Him as He *really* is, not try to make a false image of God in our mind. If we love God, we will say His name with respect and remember how great He is when we speak about Him. If we love God, we will want to set aside time to get away from the work that distracts us and remember who God is and how wonderful He is.

Questions for Your Kids:

1. Can you repeat to me the first four commandments? (*See how much your kids can remember. Be encouraging. Praise them for what they can remember. Gently remind them about what they forget.*)

2. What is the greatest commandment according to Jesus? (*To love the Lord your God with all your heart, soul, mind, and strength.*)

3. Do you think you love God this way? (*If your child says yes, repeat the words back to him or her, emphasizing the word "all." We do not love God with all our hearts because we still sin. Even when we believe in Christ, we still struggle with sin.*)

4. Can you think of someone who does love God this way? (*Jesus. He is the only one who has ever loved the Father perfectly. This is why, even though we fail at loving God, we don't need to fear His judgment, because the perfect Man died for the sins of the world. He has paid the price for our sin.*)

Prayer: (Start your prayer by reading Psalm 119:65-72.)
Thank you for sending Jesus, who perfectly loved You and came down from heaven to obey Your will (John 6:38). Thank you that He became obedient to death, even death on a cross (Philippians 2:8). Inspire us to love You the way He does. We delight in Your law. Amen.

LESSON 12:
The Fifth Commandment (Part 1)

Opening Thought:

One day, little Johnny was riding in the back seat of the car and took his seatbelt off. His father told him to sit down and put his seatbelt on immediately. Johnny didn't want to do it, so he stood up. His father pulled the car over and said very firmly, "Johnny, you need to put on your seatbelt immediately. It's dangerous to ride without one." Johnny sat down and put his belt on. Then he looked at his father and said, "I may be sitting on the outside, but I'm standing up on the inside."

Think about that story as we read the fifth commandment.

Scripture Reading: Exodus 20:12 and Ephesians 6:1-3

Explanation: In the Bible, the word "father" refers not just to your dad, but also to your grandfather and great-grandfather. The word "mother" refers not just to your mom, but also to your grandmother and great-grandmother.

God wants children to honor their parents and older relatives. To honor someone means to treat someone with seriousness and value. It means to listen carefully when parents speak and to speak back respectfully. It means to obey with the right attitude.

In our story about Johnny not wearing his seatbelt, he may have finally obeyed his dad, but he still had a rebellious heart. God is just as concerned about your attitude as he is with what you do.

God is the one who placed us into families. He is one who invented moms and dads. He wants us to learn to honor our older relatives. And there's a reason for this. He says if we honor our parents, it will go well with us and we will enjoy a long life on the earth.

Why is this? First, if we honor our parents as they teach us about God, we will learn to obey God, and we will be blessed for obeying God. Second, if we learn to honor our parents when we are young, it will be easier to honor other people who are in charge of us when we are older. If we learn to honor our parents, it will be easier to honor a boss we work for in the future. We will be more likely to obey the laws in our land. We will also be more likely to obey our spiritual leaders at church.

This is why it is so important to have an attitude of respect to parents, because we will learn to obey God in everything we do and have a blessed life.

Questions for Your Kids:

1. What does it mean to honor someone? (*To treat someone with seriousness and value*)

2. What is the opposite of honor? (*Treating someone lightly, as if they don't matter*)

3. What is the promise for those who honor and obey their parents? (*The promise is that it will go well with us and we will have long life on the earth.*)

4. Have you ever dishonored an older relative before? (*Have your kids think of a time when their attitude wasn't honoring. Have your kids think about any time they argued with an adult who told them what to do. Have them talk about a time when they have obeyed an adult but did it with a bad attitude.*)

5. Why is it hard to honor parents? (*It is difficult because, in our sinfulness, we want to have our own way. When parents tell us to do something we don't want to do, we don't want to give up our plans.*)

6. Does God want you to honor your older relatives because they are perfect? (*No. That's not the reason we should obey parents and older relatives. No one is perfect. When an adult sins they should apologize and ask for forgiveness, just like when kids sin. Parents aren't in charge because they are* perfect. *They are in charge because of the One who put them in charge.*)

> # Prayer: (Start your prayer by reading Psalm 119:73-80.)
> The older generations declare to the younger all the great and mighty things you have done and sing aloud of your faithfulness and goodness (Psalm 145:4-7). You promise that the wisdom of the older generations is like a light that will lead us as we walk, watch over us while we sleep, and talk to us when we awake (Proverbs 6:20-23). You have placed us into a family, so help us to honor and listen the older generations. Amen.

Opening Thought:

Before Jesus was born as a man, He lived with His heavenly Father, right? (**See if your children know this about Christ already.**)

As the Son of God, He was involved in creating the whole world. Through Him everything was made, including people.

When Jesus came to earth as a man, since He was the Son of God, did He have to obey His earthly parents, Joseph and Mary? (**See what your kids say about this.**)

I'm going to read the fifth commandment again and then a story about Jesus. Listen to what Jesus does in this story.

Scripture Reading: Exodus 20:12 and Luke 2:40-52

Explanation: Jesus grew up like all young boys grow. He got taller, stronger, and smarter as He grew. He encountered the same kind of temptations and struggles as a child that you face.

He also grew up in a home with parents who obeyed God's law. Every year Joseph and Mary would follow God's command to go up to Jerusalem for the special feast of Passover. Every year they would walk for several days, traveling 80 miles from their home town to Jerusalem, to celebrate this feast. Every year they would spend a full week in Jerusalem celebrating and learning about God from the Jewish teachers.

When Jesus was twelve, He went with His parents to the feast. Like a good father, Joseph wanted Jesus to learn more about God and follow God's commands, so they took Him to this special feast. They traveled in a big caravan of people, meaning a large group all walked together. Typically all the kids would walk up front, followed by the women in the middle, followed by the men in the back.

When the feast was over and their caravan of people was leaving, they didn't know Jesus wasn't up front with all the other kids. They traveled a full day but couldn't find Jesus with all the other kids. So they walked back to Jerusalem, and after three days, they finally found Him in the temple. He was sitting with the Jewish teachers, eagerly listening to them, learning, asking questions, and everyone was so impressed by how much wisdom He had.

Joseph and Mary learned a lesson that day. They should have remembered who Jesus was, and they should have gone straight to the temple to find Him, because the temple was His heavenly Father's house. As Jesus was becoming a man and getting older, He knew who He was, that He was the Son of God. He didn't just have an earthly mother and father; He had a heavenly Father, and He loved his heavenly Father.

Still, the Bible says that Jesus went back to his home town with Joseph and Mary and He was submissive to them. Even though Jesus was the Son of God, even though He was the most powerful and important person ever born, He still obeyed and honored His parents. He did this because He knew God's law: honor your father and mother.

Questions for Your Kids:

1. Why do you think Joseph and Mary thought Jesus was in the caravan when they were going home? (*Because Jesus had always been obedient to them. He was their son, so they wouldn't expect Him to go anywhere else.*)

2. Why did Jesus stay in the temple? (*Because it was His heavenly Father's house and He wanted to be there.*)

3. Do you think Jesus was being dishonoring to His parents by staying in the temple? (*No. Jesus' parents hadn't told Jesus to return with them. They just mistakenly thought Jesus was with their big group.*)

4. Why would Jesus still obey His parents, even though He was the Son of God? (*Because God commanded children to honor their parents, and Jesus was obedient to God's command.*)

Prayer: (Start your prayer by reading Psalm 119:81-88.)
Thank You for sending Your Son to Earth. Thank You that He always honored His parents and obeyed Your law. Help us to honor and obey our parents in everything, because we know this pleases You (Colossians 3:20). Amen.

Opening Thought:

We're going to talk about a very serious subject today. One of God's commands is about killing.

Why do you think people kill one another? (*See what reasons your children give to you. Ask them what kind of thoughts must go through someone's mind before they murder someone else.*)

Think about those things as we read the sixth commandment and what Jesus said about the sixth commandment.

Scripture Reading: Exodus 20:13 and Matthew 5:21-22

Explanation: This commandment is not talking about *all* kinds of killing. There are at least eight different words for killing in the Bible, but this commandment uses only one of those words. It isn't talking about killing in war, or killing an animal, or putting someone to death because they broke a law. It is talking about if you plan to murder someone and then you do. It is also talking about if you get in a fight with someone and you kill them during the struggle. God doesn't want anyone to die this way.

Jesus agrees and says, yes, we should never murder, but asks us to also think about what causes someone to murder another person. It is often motivated out of anger. When you get angry at someone in a sinful way, it comes out in the way you treat them, in the way you talk to them or about them. We might call someone a bad name. We might treat them poorly or with a mean spirit. If our anger gets bad enough, sometimes people will even kill one another.

Anger is not always wrong. The Bible says that even God gets angry. But He always gets angry about the right things and shows it in the right way. When we get angry, we often get angry about the wrong things, about things we selfishly want. When we get angry, we often show it in the wrong way: we show a large amount of anger for a small thing. When we get angry, we don't always have self-control. God is always in control of Himself, but often when we get angry we are overcome by our passions and are out of control.

Anger is more than an emotion. When we get angry in a sinful way, we are really focused on someone who is against us, and we feel a need to respond in an intense way. We may never murder people with our hands, but we do murder people with our words. We begin to treat others like enemies. We insist that we are right and everyone else is wrong, so we hurt others with what we say and do.

Questions for Your Kids:

1. Can you think of a time when you were really angry about something and it showed by the way you spoke? (*Help your kids remember the last time they shouted something in anger or when they spoke an unkind word.*)

2. Do you remember what made you angry? (*Help your kids think of the event. Most likely, it was something that wasn't going their way, so they got mad.*)

3. Compare the size of the problem you had with the size of your anger. Did the problem require you to show that much anger? (*Often what makes anger sinful is how large it is in comparison to the offense. Model for your kids the kind of response you think they should have had at that moment.*)

4. Have you ever been angry and found it hard to calm down? (*Help your kids remember times when they were angry and had a hard time calming down.*)

5. Why is it so easy to get angry? (*Because sometimes we want something to happen so much, if a person gets in the way of that, we get mad at that person. In our sin, we treasure things happening our own way more than we treasure the other person. Parents, talk to your kids about what easily makes you lash out in anger.*)

Prayer: (Start your prayer by reading Psalm 119:89-96.)
Help us to remember Your precepts, because by them we have life. Tame our angry hearts and mouths. With the same mouth we praise You and then we angrily curse people who are made in Your image. It should not be this way (James 3:7-10). Set up a guard for our mouth; keep watch at the door of our lips. Do not let our hearts turn to any evil thing (Psalm 141:3). Amen.

Opening Thought:

What do you remember about the sixth commandment? (*See what your children remember about what was learned in the lesson prior.*)

The commandment is about not killing, but when Jesus explained the commandment, he said it is also about where murder comes from in our hearts. We need to watch our hearts carefully to make sure we aren't getting sinfully angry.

What is the opposite of being angry at someone? (*The opposite of anger is showing love, compassion, gentleness, and kindness, even when someone might be doing something offensive to us.*)

What is the opposite of murder? (*The opposite of murder is doing what we can to preserve and defend our life and the lives of others.*)

Think about that as we read this story about Jesus.

Scripture Reading: Mark 5:22-43

Explanation: While there are times in Jesus' life when He got angry, He never got angry in a sinful way. Usually, He was the opposite of angry. Instead of hurting others with his words, He spoke with compassion. Instead of striking to hit others or hurt them, He used His power to heal and even bring others back to life.

This is a story of two miracles. While Jesus was on His way to the home of a very important religious leader to heal his daughter, a woman with a terrible disease saw Him walking by with a crowd of people. She believed He had the power to heal her, so she reached out and grabbed the hem of His robe. Power came from Jesus, through His robe, and instantly healed her. After He felt the power go out of Himself, He stopped the crowd to look for the woman who touched Him. He wanted to speak to the person who was healed. When He saw the woman, He spoke words of compassion to her and told her to go in peace.

Arriving at the religious leader's home, they find out his sick daughter has just died. Everyone thought it was too late. He spoke words of reassurance to the father, telling him not to fear. He brought everyone out of the room. He held the dead girl's hand and commanded her to rise up, and she was immediately healed. He raised her from the dead.

At different times in this story, Jesus could have gotten angry. He could have been annoyed that the woman touched his garment without asking. He could have been impatient because she had interrupted Him while He was on the way to a very important man's house. But He didn't. Instead, He spoke words of tenderness and kindness to her. He spoke reassuring words to those who mourned the death of the little girl. When the crowd laughed at Him, He didn't get angry with them. Jesus chose to use His great power to heal others, not harm them. Instead of taking life, He brought people back to life and healed their bodies.

Questions for Your Kids:

1. When someone interrupts your plans, is it easy to get impatient with them? (*Yes. When we have plans, it is easy be frustrated when people interrupt us. We have to remember that people are usually more important than our plans.*)

2. When people make fun of us, is it easy to get mad at them? (*Yes. We don't want people to tease us or laugh at us. We have to remember that lashing back at them is not the answer.*)

3. Did Jesus always obey the sixth commandment? (*Yes. He didn't just refrain from killing people; He did the opposite. He gave people their lives back. He healed. He spoke with kind and compassionate words.*)

Prayer: (Start your prayer by reading Psalm 119:97-104.)
Thank You for sending Your Son to us to show us what compassion looks like. Jesus never turned aside from Your law, because You were His teacher. In the same way, give us Your wisdom from above. Let it show through our purity, our peaceful spirit, our gentleness, mercy, and sincerity. Drive out all jealousy and selfish ambition that would cause us to sin in anger (James 3:13-18). Amen.

CHRIST IN THE COMMANDMENTS
A family study of the 10 Commandments

LESSON 16:
The Seventh
Commandment
(Part 1)

Opening Thought:

Have you ever seen two married people who are really in love? (*Have your children think about the married couples they know who show affection for each other. Perhaps they think of you and your spouse, their grandparents, or a couple they know at church.*)

How do you think one of them would feel if his or her spouse went out and started dating other people? (*That person would be very sad and jealous.*)

Think about that as we read the seventh commandment and Jesus' teaching about it.

Scripture Reading: Exodus 20:14 and Matthew 5:27-30

Explanation: Men and women were designed by God to love each other and get married. Someday, if you are called to get married, you may find someone that you want to serve and love for the rest of your life. When people get married, they show their love to each other in many ways: kissing, hugging, talking to each other, spending time together, sleeping together at night, and even having children together. When you are married, the Bible says you become "one flesh" with that person: you are united together for life.

But what would happen if your spouse decided they wanted to act like they were married to someone else too? What if they started going out on dates with someone else? Spending a lot of time with that person? Hugging and kissing that person? This would be very unsettling, because marriage is supposed to be between one man and one woman. When people sin this way, it is called adultery.

But just like we talked about with anger, adultery doesn't start with our actions; it starts in our hearts and in our thoughts. Before someone commits adultery, they first imagine it in their mind. They see someone who catches their attention and they start imagining what it would be like to be with that person, to be loved by that person. Jesus says this is like committing adultery in the heart.

This is why, before we get married, we need to careful about how we think about people of the opposite sex. There will come a day when it will be the right time for you to think about getting married. But until that time, with every boy or girl you meet, you should think about them like a brother or sister. Treat them with respect. Don't imagine yourself acting like their husband or wife.

The same thing is true about pictures of people we see in magazines or in movies or in TV shows. Don't start imagining yourself acting like you're married to that person. God wants us to save those thoughts for the person to whom we get married.

Questions for Your Kids:

1. Who created marriage? (*God*)

2. Is marriage a good thing? (*Yes. God invented marriage. This is why He made men and women.*)

3. If you are married, should you date someone else, too? (*No. This would be adultery.*)

4. Before you are married, should you act like or pretend that you are married to someone? (*No.*)

Prayer: (Start your prayer by reading Psalm 119:105-112.)

Even when there is a snare of temptation in front of us, help us not to stray from Your law. We do not want to put any worthless thing before our eyes (Psalm 101:3). Help us to treat older men as fathers, younger men as brothers, older women as mothers, and younger women as sisters (1 Timothy 5:1-2). Help us to become the kind of people who will be good husbands or wives.

Opening Thought:

Did Jesus ever get married when He was on earth? (*No.*)

Did Jesus ever commit adultery, acting like He was in love with a woman? (*No. Jesus was sinless.*)

Think about that today as we read the seventh commandment again and another passage about Jesus.

Scripture Reading: Exodus 20:14 and Ephesians 5:22-33

Explanation: In this passage Jesus is likened to a groom and His people, the church, are likened to a bride, the one who will be married to Jesus. Though Jesus was never married when He was here on Earth, He will be married to the church.

The Bible says Christ is the **head** of the church. This doesn't mean Jesus is bossy or prideful or dominating. It means that with all His great power and authority, He serves the church in love. Jesus served His followers when He was here on Earth, and He served the whole church by being willing to die for our sins on the cross. Jesus was the ultimate servant.

Being the head of the church also means He leads the church. He teaches us through the Scriptures. He sets the perfect example for us. He is always with us. He even gives us a share of His authority and teaches us to lead others.

Jesus is 100% faithful to the church. He has always loved the church with a perfect love. He not only died for the church, He continues to nourish and cherish the church, making us more and more into a perfect bride.

This the kind of love husbands should have for their wives. They should not only teach them, spend time with them, and lead them by example, but be willing to lay down their lives for their wives. Similarly, a good wife will affirm the way her husband leads by honoring him and supporting him.

Obeying the seventh commandment is not just about not committing adultery. It is about being 100% faithful to the person you are married to. It means being the kind of person that will love, honor, and serve your spouse your whole life.

Questions for Your Kids:

1. Do you think you will get married some day? (*See what your children say. Ultimately, no one but God knows if your children will grow up and get married. Affirm to your kids both the goodness of being married and being single.*)

2. Regardless of whether you get married or not, you want to be the kind of person who would love your spouse. Who is the ultimate example of love? (*Jesus*)

3. What does it mean to be faithful to your spouse? (*It means not committing adultery, but it also means loving him or her the way Christ loves us. It means serving someone in love. Parents, if you are married, talk to your kids about the way your spouse serves and loves you.*)

Prayer: (Start your prayer by reading Psalm 119:113-120.)
Thank You for creating marriage. Prepare us to be the kind of people who will be good husbands and wives, to love and honor our future spouse the right way. When You join people together in marriage, let no one tear them apart (Matthew 19:6). You have called us to holiness, not impurity (1 Thessalonians 4:7). Help us to be faithful to You and Your law. Amen.

Opening Thought:

Have you ever had something stolen from you? (*Have your kids think if anything has ever been taken from them.*)

How do you think it feels if something is taken from you? (*Have your kids describe the disappointment, sadness, anger, or frustration someone might feel.*)

Today, we're going to read the eighth commandment and another text from the New Testament about stealing.

Scripture Reading: Exodus 20:15 and Hebrews 13:5-6

Explanation: Stealing is when you take something away from one else that doesn't belong to you. Instead of stealing, the Bible tells us to work hard so we have something to share with those in need. We should never want to take what isn't ours, but instead we should desire to *give* to others.

There are many ways we can steal from someone else.
- Some people buy or receive things they know are stolen from other people. This is stealing because they are helping out the thief.
- Some people lie to others to get them to buy things they don't need.
- Some people buy things with their credit card but never pay the bill.
- Some steal from the people they work for by not working a full day when they say they did: this takes money from their boss that they didn't earn.
- Some don't steal money, but they steal other things, like when they are taking a test in school and they cheat by copying someone else's answers. This is stealing another person's hard work.

Stealing is offensive to God because God is the one who provides for our needs. When we take something that isn't ours, we are saying in our hearts, "I don't care if God gave this thing to someone else. I want it. I think God should have given it to me."

Instead, we should be content with the things we have. We shouldn't love money or things so much that we feel compelled to steal from others. God promises, "I will never leave you nor forsake you." If we trust that He is always with us and will always take care of us, we have no reason to steal from others. God will meet our needs.

Questions for Your Kids:

1. Have you ever really wanted something that someone else had? (*Have your kids talk about something their friend or sibling has they really want.*)

2. Have you ever wanted something so much you thought about it all the time? (*This begins to get into the sin of covetousness, but have your kids talk about a time when they remember thinking about obsessing over something they really wanted.*)

3. If we need something or want something, what is the appropriate way of getting it? (*We should pray to God for what we need. We also need to work for the money we need if we're going to buy it.*)

Prayer: (Start your prayer by reading Psalm 119:121-128.)

We love Your commandments more than the finest gold. Never let us experience great poverty where we are tempted to steal from others and profane Your name. Never let us be tempted by riches so that we forget You (Proverbs 30:7-9). Help us to do honest work with our own hands so we never steal from anyone, but rather give to those in need (Ephesians 4:28). Amen.

Opening Thought:

What is the opposite of stealing? (*The opposite of stealing is giving to those in need.*)

If we do steal from others, how should we apologize to them? (*We should give more than an apology. We should give back what we stole.*)

In today's story we'll read about a man who met Jesus who did just that.

Scripture Reading: Luke 19:1-10

Explanation: The people in Jesus' day did not like tax collectors. These were people who worked for the Roman government, taking taxes from people to give to the empire. People didn't like paying the Roman government, but they really disliked tax collectors because they were known for charging people *more* than what they owed. This is what made them rich. Zacchaeus wasn't just any tax collector; he was a chief tax collector, which means he was the boss of other tax collectors. He was very wealthy and very disliked by others because he was a thief.

He was also really short. Can you picture him in this big crowd of people who are looking at Jesus as He passes through the city of Jericho? Can you picture him bouncing up and down trying to get a good look at Jesus because he's too short to see Him? Finally, Zacchaeus climbs up into a sycamore tree to get a better look.

But Jesus stopped at the tree and called up to Zacchaeus, inviting Himself over to his house. He wanted to be Zacchaeus' guest. Immediately, the whole crowd was shocked. Why would Jesus spend time with a sinner like Zacchaeus? Everyone hated him because he was a thief, but Jesus wanted to spend time with him. Why?

We do not know what Jesus spoke about with Zacchaeus that day, but after spending time with Jesus, everything changed in his heart. First, he hated that he had stolen so much money, so he promised to give back to anyone from whom he stole money. He would give them *four times the amount* he stole from them. So if Zacchaeus had stolen $100 from you, he would have given you back $400. He also promised to give half of everything he owned to the poor. This mean Zacchaeus might have given away nearly everything he owned. Meeting Jesus had totally changed this man's heart.

Jesus tells the disciples that this is why he wanted to come to Zacchaeus' house: His mission was to seek and save those who are lost in sin. By spending time with Zacchaeus and becoming his friend, Zacchaeus was saved. His life was changed forever.

Questions for Your Kids:

1. How did Jesus know Zacchaeus' name? (*Maybe He had heard about Zacchaeus before. Maybe Jesus knew him because of His supernatural power. There are many times Jesus knows the hearts of people without them even speaking to them.*)

2. Why do you think Zacchaeus was willing to give away so much of his money? (*Because first he wanted to make things right with the people from whom he stole money. Second, he wanted to become a giver, not a taker. He wanted to share his wealth with those in need.*)

3. By coming over to Zacchaeus' home, what was Jesus trying to say to Zacchaeus? (*To enter into someone's home showed that you wanted to be their friend. Jesus didn't care what other people thought about Zacchaeus. He wanted Zacchaeus to be saved from his sin.*)

Prayer: (Start your prayer by reading Psalm 119:129-136.)

We don't want to steal from others. We want to be givers. Forgive us when we think only about ways we can **keep** our money and buy things only for ourselves. You love a cheerful giver. Help us to want to give our money, not because we have to, but out of love for others (2 Corinthians 9:7). Amen.

Opening Thought:

Have you ever heard of a white lie? (*See if your kids know what that expression means.*)

A white lie is a lie that doesn't seem like a big deal. People tell white lies when they think they have good intentions. For instance, what if someone compliments you on something you did, but you actually didn't really do it. Someone else did it, but you like getting the compliment. So you say, "Thank you," but you never tell the person that you didn't do it. That would be a kind of white lie.

What do you think? Is telling a white lie a sin? (*See what your kids say before you read the passage aloud to them.*)

Scripture Reading: Exodus 20:16 and Proverbs 6:16-19

Explanation: The Lord hates lies. God wants us to tell the truth, even when the truth might harm us.

Think about the example of the white lie. If people are mistaken and say something that isn't right but we don't correct them, that is a type of lie. We're letting people believe something that is false.

If we say something that is mostly true, but we mix in a lie, that is also lying. If you are asked to clean your room, and you clean most of it but not all of it, and then you are asked, "Did you clean your room?" What should you say? You should say, "No, I have not cleaned all of it." We shouldn't lie and give the impression that it is totally clean.

If we hear something about someone else that is embarrassing, instead of listening to it and then sharing it with others, we should stop people and say, "Let's not talk about this. We don't even know if this is true."

We want to be people of truth. If we hear something that is false, we should correct it, and we should never say anything that isn't true to others.

Questions for Your Kids:

1. Can you think of a time when you told a lie? (*Perhaps your kids will remember a time when they told a lie, even a small one. If not, help them to remember a time when they did this. Also, tell them about a time when you lied.*)

2. Why do you think people lie? (*People lie usually because they have something to gain from lying. Often, people lie because they can get something they want. If they lie about something they haven't done, but they say they did it, this makes them look good in other people's eyes. If they lie about someone they don't like, they do it to hurt that person's reputation.*)

3. If you lie but no one else finds out about it, who will always know about it? (*God. He sees and knows everything.*)

Prayer: (Start your prayer by reading Psalm 119:137-144.)
We know the mouths of all liars will be stopped some day (Psalm 63:11). No one who practices deceit or tells lies can be in Your house (Psalm 101:7). Help us to learn to speak truth in love to others (Ephesians 4:15). Amen.

Opening Thought:

If you were on trial for telling a lie, do you think you would be found guilty? (*Have your kids think about any time they ever lied.*)

If everyone who ever knew you were questioned about whether you ever lied, do you think eventually someone would say that you lied to them? (*Yes. Eventually someone will come forward who remembers a time when you lied to them.*)

This wouldn't be true for Jesus. Let's read this story about when Jesus was on trial.

Scripture Reading: 1 Peter 2:21-25

Explanation: Peter, one of Jesus' most famous disciples, is writing this letter. He's remembering the time when Jesus was on trial, right before He was crucified. Peter was there and saw a lot of it happen.

Peter talks about how Jesus suffered physically. He mentions Jesus' wounds, the nails that pierced His hands and feet, the spear that stabbed His side, and the terrible whips that took flesh from His back. He says Jesus bore our sins in His body on the cross. He felt terrible physical pain because He was dying in our place, for our sins.

Peter says Jesus suffered not only from how people *hurt* Him, but from what they *said* to Him. At His trial, they criticized His ministry. They called Him a liar and a criminal. They threatened Him. They mocked Him and made fun of Him. They lied about the things He had said and done. Many of the witnesses they got at His trial were actually breaking the ninth commandment by lying about the things He said and did.

But Jesus did not respond like most people would respond. He didn't yell back. He didn't criticize them. He didn't lie to defend Himself. For most of the trial, He said nothing at all. He had a quiet confidence about Him. Peter could see from the look on His face: their threats didn't scare Him. He was trusting completely in His Father. He didn't need to lie or yell or use words to intimidate them. He had the power to calm a thunder storm or call 100,000 angels to His side with just one word, but He stayed silent and trusted God.

Questions for Your Kids:

1. During His trial, how did the witnesses break the ninth commandment? (*They lied about the things Jesus said and did.*)

2. During His trial, how did Jesus obey the ninth commandment? (*Jesus stood for truth. When He spoke, He spoke the truth. He was sincere and spoke clearly. He didn't lie to defend Himself.*)

3. If someone was telling lies about you, how would that make you feel? (*Have your children tell you how it would hurt their feelings.*)

4. Do you think it would have been tempting to yell back or get angry if you were in Jesus' place? (*Yes. We all probably would have wanted to try to defend ourselves if we were being lied about.*)

Prayer: (Start your prayer by reading Psalm 119:145-152.)
Men gathered around Jesus to persecute Him, but He stayed true to Your word. We know that out of the overflow of our hearts our mouths speak (Luke 6:45). Help us to have a heart like Jesus' heart. We want to tell the truth all the time. Sanctify us though the truth. Your word is truth (John 17:17). Amen.

Opening Thought:

Can you think of something that a friend of yours has that you would really like to have? (*Have your kids talk about a toy or game or pet or object a friend of theirs owns.*)

When you go to the store, do you ever see things on the shelves and wish you could have them? (*Have your kids talk about the last time they went to the store and really wanted to buy something.*)

Think about that feeling you have when you really, really want something. As you think about this, we're going to read the tenth commandment and another passage from the New Testament.

Scripture Reading: Exodus 20:17 and 1 Timothy 6:6-10

Explanation: There are two words here to pay attention to: covet and content. God says we should never **covet** something our neighbor has. The word covet means to be jealous about something that someone else has. Coveting is a strong desire to get something that isn't ours. The opposite of this is to be **content**. Contentment is to be happy with what God has given you.

Think about the world we live in today. If you turn on the TV, you'll see commercials trying to get you to buy the newest toy. If you walk in the store, you'll see thousands of signs telling you to buy new things. It seems everywhere you go in the world, something is trying to tell us we need to get something newer or better. The Bible says to be very careful not to get so wrapped up in money and the stuff it can buy.

Think about a boat on the water. The boat needs water to float from one side of the lake to the other. The water is necessary for the boat to move. But if water starts flooding into the boat, it will sink. It's the same way with money and possessions. Money is good. Possessions are good. We need them to get along in this world. But when we want things of this world so much that it consumes our thoughts, this is called covetousness. When we want money or possessions so much that they flood our hearts, we stop thinking about God and His kingdom.

A boat in the water is good; water in the boat is bad. Having money is good; money taking control of our hearts is bad.

Always wanting more and more is a trap. Even if we get something new and fun, eventually we will get bored with it, and we'll want something new. Then we get that new thing, have it for a while, get bored, and want something new. It's like we can never be satisfied. When we spend all our time thinking about getting more money or new things, we forget the things that are most important. We forget about God.

Questions for Your Kids:

1. Can you think of something you believe you have coveted that you saw at the store or at a friend's house? (*The point here is to think of an example of an overwhelming desire your child has had for something new, something that seemed to consume his or her thoughts.*)

2. If tomorrow we suddenly moved to a smaller house, and almost all your clothes were gone, all your toys were gone, and we didn't have any money to buy new toys, how would you feel? (*Get your children to really think what it would be like to have only a few possessions: enough food and clothing, but nothing much more. Would they be content or would they think about their old house and their old toys all the time? Give them example of some of their favorite possessions and what it would be like not to have them.*)

Prayer: (Start your prayer by reading Psalm 119:153-160.)
Life is not about the abundance of things we possess (Luke 12:15). We confess that we covet things that are not ours. We are greedy for things of this world. Teach us the secret of being content in any circumstance. Teach us the secret of being content, whether we have plenty or we do not. We can do all things through You who gives us strength (Philippians 4:11-13). Amen.

Opening Thought:

Last time we read the tenth commandment. Can you remember what the tenth commandment is about? (**See how much your kids can remember.**)

What is different about the tenth commandment from all the others is that it focuses on the heart. All the other commandments, of course, have to do with our hearts, but this commandment talks directly about our heart and our desires. This commandment doesn't focus on what we do but on what we want and desire.

Think about that as we read part of a letter from the apostle Paul.

Scripture Reading: Romans 7:7-9, 18-25

Explanation: In this passage, the apostle Paul is telling a story about a time when he was young and he was reading God's commandments. It was probably when he was a kid, maybe even your age. As he was learning the Bible, he got to the tenth commandment about not coveting, and something happened. He started thinking about all the things he wanted that he didn't have. The commandment was telling him, "Don't covet," but as soon as he read that, he realized how much he coveted other people's things.

Paul wanted to do what was right. He wanted to follow God's law. He wanted to do good. But no matter what, he always found more sin inside him. He could tell himself to be content. He could try not to covet. But before he knew it, his heart was coveting something else.

Paul says it felt like he was at war with himself. On one hand, he delighted in the law of God in his heart, but he felt this other desire in himself that wanted to be sinful. Finally, Paul cries out, "Wretched man that I am!" He was tired of being at war with himself. He wanted the war to be over. He wanted to be able to obey God completely.

Paul asks the most important question, "When we read God's law and we find we are unable to follow it, who will rescue us from ourselves? Who will rescue us from our sinful desires? Who will make us completely new so we don't have a desire to sin anymore?" Paul answers the question: God through Jesus Christ will do it. Christ can make us completely new on the inside, and someday, He will return to Earth and make us completely new on the outside as well. It is then that the war will be over.

Questions for Your Kids:

1. Have you ever been reading the Bible or listening to the Bible and thought, "I don't want to do what the Bible is telling me. I want to do my own thing"? (*Your children might confess that they've experienced this. If not, have them think about the previous lesson about coveting. See if they can remember how it felt when they were told they shouldn't covet something they really want.*)

2. One of the purposes of reading these Ten Commandments is to show us just how sinful we are. Have you ever thought about the idea that you have a war going on inside yourself? (*See if your children can identify with the idea of a sinful desire at war with a good desire.*)

3. Can we stop coveting or sinning by trying harder? (*No. Trying harder does not make sin go away.*)

4. Who can rescue us from our sin? (*Jesus*)

Prayer: (Start your prayer by reading Psalm 119:161-168.)

We know it is from within our hearts that evil thoughts and covetous desire come (Mark 7:21-22). It is easy to become so overloaded with concerns of this world. Jesus, rescue us from our sins. Thank you for your law that shows us how much we need a Savior. Amen.

Opening Thought:

How many commandments did God speak out loud to the Israelites at Mount Sinai? (*Ten*)

It can be tough to keep all of God's commandments in mind all of the time. This is why God helps us by summarizing for us what He wants us to do. Listen to what the apostle Paul wrote about the Ten Commandments.

Scripture Reading: Romans 13:8-12

Explanation: The first four of the Ten Commandments have to do with how we love God. If we love God we will worship Him alone, we will worship Him the right way, we will never take his name in vain, and we will rest from our labor so we can remember Him.

The last six commandments can be summed up with one law: Love your neighbor as yourself. In the Bible, your neighbor isn't just the person who lives next door to you. Your neighbor is *anyone* you meet.

Think about each of the last six commandments and how they all relate to loving your neighbor.

Commandment #5: Honor your parents. If we love our neighbor, this includes our parents and elders. We will not disobey them, but instead we will honor them the way they should be honored if we love them.

Commandment #6: Do not murder. If we love our neighbor, we will not harm them. We will not speak poorly about them. We will not get angry with them in a sinful way. If we love them we will do good to them instead.

Commandment #7: Do not commit adultery. If we love our neighbor, this includes our wife or husband. We will be faithful to that person if we love them. We will also not try to steal away our neighbor's spouse.

Commandment #8: Do not steal. If we love our neighbor, we won't take what belongs to them. Instead we will give to others in need if we really love them.

Commandment #9: Do not give a false witness. If we love our neighbor, we will never lie about them. We will tell the truth about ourselves and others.

Commandment #10: Do not covet. If we love our neighbor, we will not wish to have their possessions. We will be content, even if our neighbor has more than we do. If we love them, we will be happy that they have been given nice possessions.

Love does no wrong to a neighbor.

Questions for Your Kids:

1. Can you remember the last six commandments? (*See if your children can list them in order.*)

2. How can we summarize the last six commandments? What law summarizes all of them? (*Love your neighbor as yourself.*)

3. Who is your neighbor? (*Anyone you meet*)

4. Which of the last six commandments do you think is the hardest to obey? (*They are all impossible to obey perfectly, but ask your children which one really sticks out to them. Find out what they feel convicted about.*)

5. How does that commandment relate to the command to love your neighbor? (*See if your kids can remember the connection between the commandment they just mentioned and the command to love.*)

Prayer: (Start your prayer by reading Psalm 119:169-176.)
Your law is fulfilled in one word: Love your neighbor as yourself (Galatians 5:14). This is your supreme, royal law (James 2:8). Everything in the Bible depends on these laws: loving You and loving our neighbor (Matthew 22:34-40). Help us to obey with all our heart, soul, mind, and strength. Amen.

Opening Thought:

Can you remember back to when we started studying the Ten Commandments? The whole nation of Israel was camped at the base of Mount Sinai, and God told them He was going to visit them there. Do you remember what they saw and heard that day? (*See how much your kids can remember about the first lesson. Remind them about the amazing things Israel saw: how they washed their clothes and prepared themselves for three days, the boundary markers around the mountain, the lightning, thunder, dark clouds, fire consuming the mountaintop, smoke, the sound of the trumpet, the land shaking, the people shaking from terror, and then the booming voice of God.*)

Keep that in mind as we read what happened right after God was finished giving them the Ten Commandments.

Scripture Reading: **Exodus 20:18-21**

Explanation: Often we think it would be great if God would speak to us directly. We read His words in the Bible and we think, "I like that God gave us this book, but I would love to hear Him talk **out loud** to me." But that day at Mount Sinai, the people were not eager to hear God talk more. God's presence was so powerful, they were terrified. They didn't want to hear more of God's voice. His words and power were so great, they were afraid they would die.

This is the kind of God we serve. The Bible speaks of God as a consuming fire, completely holy and more powerful than we can imagine. God was giving them a small taste of that power so they could see just how big He is.

But there are two ways we can fear God. We can be frightened of God because we believe He's going to destroy us, or we can be so in awe of God so that we want to obey Him. This is what Moses says to the people: "Do not be afraid. God has come here so that you might fear Him." God had not come to kill them with His power but to teach them about how amazing He is so they would desire to obey Him and not sin.

Remember God's first words to them: "I am the Lord your God, who brought you out of the land of Egypt, out of the house of slavery." These are not the words of an angry God ready to strike them dead, but a loving God who rescued them and has made them His own people. God had come to instruct them, not destroy them.

Questions for Your Kids:

1. Have you ever thought about how big and powerful God is? If you were standing there at Mount Sinai, how do you think you would have felt? (*See how your children react. Remind them about how everyone reacted: they shook with fear.*)

2. Do you think God is still just as big and powerful today as He was then? (*Yes. God never changes. He has always been mighty and great.*)

3. When God comes to judge the world, do you think people will be frightened? (*Yes, and they should be. The Bible said it is a fearful thing to fall into the hands of the living God.*)

4. Should Christians be frightened that God is going to condemn us? (*No. If we are united to Christ, we are not condemned. We are God's own children.*)

5. What's the difference between being *terrified* of God and *fearing* God? (*It is the difference between being terrified of God's judgment and fearing God in a way that makes us want to obey Him because He is worthy of obedience.*)

Prayer: You gathered Your people at Sinai that day to so we would learn to fear You all the days of our lives, and so we would teach our children to fear You as well (Deuteronomy 4:10). All the ends of the earth will fear you (Psalm 67:7). Who can be compared to You? Who is as mighty as You are? You calm the storms at sea and crush all Your enemies. The whole world is Yours. You have made it all. You are righteous, just, loving, and faithful. You are feared greatly, even by the angels in heaven (Psalm 89:5-14). Help us to stand in awe of You. Amen.

Opening Thought:

Let's say we had a lot of chores to do and I wanted you to help me. Let's say I started saying all those chores out loud so you knew what to do, but as I talked, the list of things got really long. Do you think you could easily remember everything I told you? (*Not easily. I would be difficult to remember a long list.*)

What would help you to remember all your chores? (*See if your kids can come up with a solution. The best way would be to write them down so you don't forget.*)

That's what God did for us. He didn't just tell us His law out loud. He wrote it down for us. I'm going to read some words from Moses. He is speaking to the people about what happened at Mount Sinai when they received the Ten Commandments.

Scripture Reading: Deuteronomy 4:5-14

Explanation: Moses says that God wrote down the Ten Commandments on two tablets of stone. After God spoke the Ten Commandments out loud, Moses went up Mount Sinai into the thick darkness where God was. There God gave Moses more laws for Israel to obey. While he was on the mountain, God gave Moses a special gift. God wrote with His finger on two tablets of stone (Exodus 31:18). On each tablet God wrote down the Ten Commandments—two copies.

Just like when you buy something at the store or when you sign an important document: you get a copy and the other person gets a copy. God had made a covenant, a special relationship with them, and now Israel and God each had a copy of God's rules written down so they would never forget them.

For God, it was important to write down His words. The Ten Commandments are special, because God Himself wrote them on stone tablets, but they aren't the only time God had His words written down. He inspired other people to write His words down. He spoke to Moses and Moses wrote the words of the first five books of the Bible. Then other prophets came along who were given the power to hear God speak, and they wrote down God's words. Men like Isaiah, Jeremiah, Ezekiel, and Daniel were great prophets who wrote books in our Bible. God gave words to others who wrote about the history of Israel, the Psalms, and other books of wisdom. He inspired men to write down the things Jesus did and said. God's Spirit even taught them about what will happen at the end of the age when Jesus returns.

All of these writings are compiled in the Bible, and this is why the Bible is the most important book on Earth. They are a record of God's words, God's message to us.

Questions for Your Kids:

1. What do you think the tablets of stone looked like? (*We really don't know what they looked like, but it is fun to imagine.*)

2. Why do you think God wrote down His words for us rather than just speaking them out loud to someone? (*God did speak out loud at Mount Sinai, but He wanted His people to always remember His words. So He wrote them down so they could be passed on from one generation to the next. He also wrote them down so we could study them.*)

3. Why is the Bible the most important book on earth? (*Because it is God's inspired Word. No other book is inspired like the Bible is.*)

4. How should we treat the Bible? (*We should be eager to read it and listen to it because it is full of God's words and God's thoughts. We should also be eager to share the words of the Bible with others.*)

Prayer: Your Word is truth (John 17:17). Every stroke of the pen from the writers of the Bible was inspired by You, and not one stroke will pass away until You have fulfilled every promise You wrote (Matthew 5:18). Let Your word dwell in us richly (Colossians 3:17). Just like You wrote Your word on tablets of stone, write Your word on our hearts (Jeremiah 31:33). Teach us how to meditate on Your written words day and night. Amen.

LESSON 27:
The Knowledge of Sin

Opening Thought:

Let's see how many of the Ten Commandments you can remember. Name some of them for me. (*See how many commandments your family can recite.*)

What would you say are the toughest commandments to obey? (*See if your children can name even one commandment that is difficult for them to obey.*)

Think about that as we read this letter from the apostle Paul about God's law.

Scripture Reading: Romans 3:10-26

Explanation: Paul makes it pretty clear: when you read God's law and see what God demands of us, there isn't a person on earth who obeys Him. No one does the good things mentioned in the Ten Commandments. Paul says that no one seeks God with his whole heart. No one lives a righteous life. We all have fallen short of God's glory. This means we all don't give God the glory and worship He should get. Every time we fail to obey God, we treat God as if He isn't important.

Think about just a few examples:
- We break the first commandment when we worship other things more than God. Many times, something else is our greatest treasure in life, not God.
- We break the fifth commandment whenever we don't respect and obey our parents, or even when we obey them, but with a bad attitude. When we don't honor our parents, we are saying to God, "I don't care that you gave me parents to honor. I don't want to do it."
- We break the sixth commandment whenever we get angry at a person for the wrong reason, when we are mean to them, or when our anger is out of control. We're putting our own selfish desires before someone else who is made in the image of God. This dishonors God.
- We break the tenth commandment any time we aren't content with what we own, or when we have a strong desire for something that someone else has. It's as if we're telling God, "I don't trust you to give me what I need," or "I don't like what you've given me in life." This dishonors God.

Sometimes we break one or more of the Ten Commandments every day. In God's eyes, everyone is guilty. You might try to obey the commandments, but you will fail.

So why would God give us the Ten Commandments if He knew we couldn't obey them? He did because He wanted to show us how much we sin. He wanted to show us that no matter how hard we try, we don't come close to being perfect. Every day of our lives, we treat ourselves as if we are more important than God.

But then Paul gives us the good news. He says we don't become right in God's sight by trying to obey the commandments more. Instead, God gives us a free gift. He counts His righteousness as ours. He totally forgives us of all our sin. He treats us as if we have always obeyed Him.

But God couldn't just ignore sin. It wouldn't be good for God to just ignore every terrible thing that people have done. Instead, His own Son, Jesus Christ, chose to be punished in our place. Instead of God being angry at us, He punished His own Son. He treated His own Son like a sinner, and now He treats us as His sons and daughters.

Questions for Your Kids:

1. Why did God give us His commandments if He knew we couldn't obey them? (*He did this to show us that we are sinners and that we need His forgiveness.*)

2. What does it mean that we have fallen short of God's glory? (*It means every time we sin, we don't give God the honor and glory and worship He should get. Every time we sin, we are telling God we would rather do what we want and not honor Him.*)

3. Do you think maybe one of the reasons why the people trembled so much at Mount Sinai is because they knew they couldn't obey the commandments God was giving them? (*Possibly, yes. They weren't just afraid of God's voice.*)

4. What did Jesus do for us on the cross? (*He died for us, choosing to be punished by His Father for our sins.*)

5. How do we become forgiven and right in God's sight? (*We have to have faith in Jesus, then God gives us His free gift of salvation.*)

Prayer: When we sin, we act as if we don't care about Your law (1 John 3:4). Thank you for giving us Your law. It shows us how much we need to be forgiven. The Ten Commandments are our guardian, our trainer; they lead us to Christ (Galatians 3:24). Thank you for sending Christ to die for our sins. Give us the faith to believe that Jesus can save all who come to Him in faith. Amen.

Opening Thought:

That day at Mount Sinai when God spoke the Ten Commandments, how loud do you think that trumpet blast was? Do you think everyone around the mountain could hear it? (*Yes. It was loud enough that everyone could hear it.*)

If you were to blow a trumpet, how long do you think you could go without taking a second breath? Try to see how long you can blow. (*Time your children. See how long they can blow by pushing air out of their lungs. Make sure they squeeze out the last bit of air they can.*)

Today we're going to read a couple short passages. The first is just a reminder about the trumpet the Israelites heard at Mount Sinai, but the second is about another time when God's trumpet will be blown.

Scripture Reading: Exodus 19:16-19 and 1 Thessalonians 4:13-18

Explanation: When you were blowing air out of your lungs, eventually you started running out of air and your breath was weaker and weaker. But when God blew the trumpet at Mount Sinai, His trumpet didn't get softer and softer. His trumpet got louder and louder. God never runs out of breath.

There's going to be another day when God will blow the trumpet again. Just like at Mount Sinai, this trumpet will announce that God the King has arrived. Only next time, He won't just be coming down on one mountain. The **whole world** will see. The next time, when the trumpet is blown, Jesus Himself will return.

The next time we hear the trumpet of God, something very special will happen to all Christians throughout the world. Those Christians who have died will rise from their graves. Their bodies will come back to life and they will rise up to be with Jesus in the air. Their bodies will be transformed into new, perfect bodies. Then those Christians who are still alive will also be changed. Their bodies will become new and perfect, and they will rise up to be with Jesus in the air. Then we will all live together on the earth and the world will be changed forever.

Jesus is going to return some day to judge the world. Some day, every person on earth will stand in front of Jesus and He will judge them according to what they did. Did they follow God's law or not? No one will be able to say they followed God's law. Everyone is guilty. God will say that those who believed in Jesus have been forgiven for all their sins, and we will all live with God forever in a new, perfect world. Those who were not forgiven will be cast out of the world and away from God forever.

When we think about Mount Sinai and the trumpet blast, it was like a rehearsal of Judgment Day. The first time God blew the trumpet, He gave us the law. The last time God will blow the trumpet, He will judge us according to that law. The important question is whether we have been *forgiven* for disobeying His law.

Questions for Your Kids:

1. Do you think everyone on Earth will be able to hear God's trumpet? (*Yes. The whole world will hear it.*)

2. What do you think our new bodies will be like? (*See what your kids will imagine about our new bodies. The Bible says they will never die or get old. They will be full of glory. They will no longer be weak but powerful [1 Corinthians 15:42-44].*)

3. Will everyone live with Jesus in the new, perfect world? (*No. Those who haven't been forgiven of their sins will be cast out of God's presence forever.*)

Prayer: Someday all your people will hear the trumpet and come to worship You on Your holy mountain (Isaiah 27:13). We will rise up and live again. Death will be swallowed up forever. We will say, "O Death, where is your victory?" (1 Corinthians 15:54-55). We look forward to that day. We pray for those who aren't forgiven. Grant them repentance (2 Timothy 2:25). Open their eyes, so that they may turn from darkness to light and from the power of Satan to God, that they may receive forgiveness of sins (Acts 26:18). Amen.

Opening Thought:

In the Old Testament, they did animal sacrifices. Do you know anything about animal sacrifices? (*See what your kids know about how animals were sacrificed by priests in the Old Testament.*)

The priests who did those sacrifices were called mediators. A mediator is someone who stands between two people to help them to work together. People would come to a priest with their animal to sacrifice. When they did, they would confess their sins over the animal and then the animal would be killed. The priest was the one who performed the sacrifice. He was the one who made sure the sacrifice was done exactly the way God wanted it to be done.

As we read this passage, think about these priests.

Scripture Reading: Hebrews 9:11-15

Explanation: God wants the people to know how serious sin is. If you had sinned back in the time of Moses, you would need to bring an animal to be sacrificed. Picture yourself bringing to a priest an animal that you've raised around your home. Then picture that animal's throat being cut open, the blood coming out, and then its body being burned on an altar. That animal is dying for your sin. Instead of God punishing you, that animal is losing its life. That's how serious sin is: it deserves death.

Only a priest was allowed to enter God's tent. On special occasions, the priests would bring the blood of animals and sprinkle that blood on the inside of God's tent. They were showing God: "See, I have performed this sacrifice. Here's the blood of the animals that have died. They have died for the sins of the people. Don't punish us for our sins."

This text calls Christ our high priest. Only He didn't enter into an earthly tent with animal blood. After He died, He went to God's real home in heaven, and He brought *His own blood* there. How much better is the blood of Jesus than the blood of animals? Jesus is the Son of God, not just another animal. He died not just for one person's sins. He died for the sins of the world.

Moses and the other priests were mediators. They performed sacrifices so the people wouldn't be punished for their sins. Christ is the perfect mediator. He was the perfect sacrifice. He had never sinned. He was the perfect Son of God. We no longer need to sacrifice animals because Jesus has paid for all of our sins.

Questions for Your Kids:

1. Why did God want Israel to sacrifice animals? (*Because sin deserves death, so these animals were dying for the sins of the people.*)

2. Did one animal ever take away all their sins for all time? (*No. They made sacrifices to God all the time. Many animals died for the sins of the people.*)

3. What is a mediator? (*A mediator is someone who stands between two people and helps them to work together. A mediator between God and man is someone who helps the people to understand what God wants, and helps the people to be right with God.*)

4. Why is Jesus the perfect mediator? (*Because He is the Son of God. He was both man and God. He was perfect. He never sinned.*)

Prayer: You are the only God, and there is only one mediator between God and man, the man Christ Jesus, who gave Himself as a ransom for all kinds of people everywhere (1 Timothy 2:5-6). Since Jesus is our great high priest who has entered the holy places of heaven, we draw near to You right now, knowing You have taken away the guilt of our sin (Hebrews 10:19-22). Thank You for sending Christ to suffer for us so that He could bring us to You (1 Peter 3:18). Amen.

Opening Thought:

Can you remember what the Israelites saw at Mount Sinai when God arrived there? (*See how much your kids can remember. Remind them about the lightning, thunder, dark clouds, fire consuming the mountaintop, smoke, the sound of the trumpet, the land shaking, the people shaking from terror, and then the boom of God's voice.*)

What do you think: Does God ever change? (*No. He does not. He does not change His mind [Number 23:19]. There's no change in Him [James 1:17].*)

This is important to understand because the God who came to Mount Sinai long ago is the same God we worship today. He is a consuming fire. He is powerful and holy. Every time we pray to Him, we should remember this. Every time we gather together for worship, we should remember this.

But even though God hasn't changed, something else *has* changed for us as Christians. Let's read what the New Testament says about this.

Scripture Reading: Hebrews 12:18-24

Explanation: The author here is talking about two different mountains. The first one he's talking about is Mount Sinai. The second one he's talking about is the heavenly mountain where God lives. He says when we gather together to pray to God or to worship Him, we are still worshipping the same God that came to Mount Sinai, but there's a big difference.

When Israel gathered at Sinai they heard the voice of God that made them tremble with fear. Even Moses was afraid. They begged that God would stop talking because they thought they would die if they heard anymore. But in heaven there is a different voice. It is the voice of Jesus. The author says Jesus who shed His blood on the cross is praying to God, and He's praying, "Father, forgive them. I have purchased them with my blood. I've paid the full price for their sins." For that reason, we don't need to be afraid like Moses and Israel were afraid.

God hasn't changed, but the difference is we know that Jesus has died for our sins. There's no boundary line keeping us away from the mountain like at Mount Sinai. There's no storm or lightning or smoke telling us to stay away. Instead there is a huge assembly of angels and the spirits of believers from the past all together worshipping God and inviting us to join them.

God is still the Judge of the whole world. But because Jesus paid the perfect sacrifice, God doesn't condemn us. He calls us His firstborn children. He calls us sons and daughters.

Some day we're going to see this heavenly mountain with our own eyes. Someday, the city of God, the new Jerusalem, is going to come from heaven to earth, we're going to see God. We're all going to gather around Him and worship Him. But until then, every time we gather together as believers to worship, we should remember we are already citizens of that city. God is not pushing us away, telling us to stay back. Even though we are all guilty, even though we have all disobeyed God's laws, Jesus has paid the price for our sin.

Questions for Your Kids:

1. Why were Moses and Israel afraid at Mount Sinai? (*Because God was showing up in a very powerful way, and they were afraid He was going to destroy them.*)

2. Should we be afraid God is going to condemn us if we come to Him? (*No. Jesus saves all who come to Him in faith. He invites all of us to come to Him.*)

3. Did God ever change? Did He stop being a judge? (*No. God is still our judge. He still judges people for their sin. But because Jesus died for our sins, He's already punished Jesus in our place.*)

4. When we pray together or get together with other believers to worship, what should our attitude be as we think about this heavenly city that we're all going to see some day? (*We should be excited and in awe of God. We don't need to fear God's punishment. But when we think about thousands of angels and believers gathered together, when we think about God the Judge on his throne, when we think about Jesus who died for us, we should be thrilled that we get to be so close to the God of the universe.*)

Prayer: We anticipate the day we will see the New Jerusalem, the day You wipe away every tear from every eye. You are making all things new (Revelation 21:1-5). Until then, help us to set our minds on things above, where Christ is seated at Your right hand (Colossians 3:1-2). Help us to remember there is no condemnation for those who are in Christ (Romans 8:1). Let the children of Zion rejoice in their King (Psalm 149:2). Amen.

ACKNOWLEDGEMENTS

I am thankful for the preaching ministry of Pastor Don Galardi. Many are grateful for his ministry at Community Evangelical Presbyterian Church that has spanned more than three decades. In particular, I am grateful for his sermon series on the Book of Exodus, which provided much thoughtful research for this book.

I am grateful for the ministers who authored the Westminster and Heidelberg catechisms. Both of these resources were instrumental in shaping the structure of this book.

Thanks to the families at Community Evangelical Presbyterian Church who prompted me to write a study for kids about the Ten Commandments.

Thanks to my wife Trisha for her daily encouragement. You make me want to be a better man.

Made in the USA
Las Vegas, NV
08 March 2022